After the

Neil Your

Published by Nine Pens

2021

www.ninepens.co.uk

ISBN: 978-1-8384321-4-0

005

In memory of my parents, Tom and Dorothy.
With thanks to my wife, Jacqueline, and our 'wean', Francine.
Big thanks as well to Hugh McMillan for the sharp-eyed edits.

Contents

Linen

You think you know your past
but then you find some things
have hidden meaning,
not just the older pictures
or your granny's watch,
the table linen
wrapped and kept for best in a drawer
but not because it waited for
a queen or star to come for tea
because it was the way the women
stitched a beauty from existence,
it made a room more than a function,
the smallest stain would be a sacrilege.

This was how the ones
who blur between the photos
blessed the next with social standing
because although
they may not own a table
they'd have the cloth.
This outlasts the repo man,
divorces, wars and emigration,
this the thread that passes
from the linen through each hand.

Dust

In time   they all stopped here:
those folk we called our family or made-up clan,
from half-a-half-cousins to uncles of aunts,
sailors and navvies with oversized yarns,
women in floral 60s skirts and head-scarves
who got their bags from the market stalls.
They wiped their feet on the front-door mat,
all their histories passed that spot
then filtered through to the living-room fire
and kitchen thick with tea and talk.
This was my mother's refuge from Orangedom,
she carried her Dickens hardbacks from Yorkshire to Belfast
as if their touch might be her last thread to a civilised world.
My father – once the latchkey kid – stood on the landing
in dripping overalls when I was born
halfway through his evening shift.
He'd ran three miles in a deluge, swerving cars and buses
from the gasworks to Ballyscillan's new estate.
Granny Lizzie arrived with a cough that stuck
like knotted rope to her lungs from 1920s TB;
my grandad like a stray dog with his whisky eyes;
his own father in final years, tramping brogues on twisted legs
that once had moved loose-knee across the Somme.
These men who tripped from war to civil war and back –
they palmed their curses onto their daughters and sons.
Here as well the priest-afflicted neighbours sang at new year,

my mother slipped them cake and clothes
in hushed insistence at the door, my brothers
larked with me in Liverpool shirts for our first Kodacolour snap.
And then, as fleet as shadows, they were gone
though they brought all this land's fierce history to a single spot:
half myth, half real, troublesome and warm, too proud and fast
to grievance, garrulous and thrawn, god-drunk and heathen,
intoxicating with their strange lyric tongue. I hold them
bitter-sweet as a song I did not know I'd memorised, though
forty years have passed since anyone kicked the carpet dust
and I am all of that house that now is left.

Barefoot Boy on V.E. Day

Wilton Street, Shankill Road, Belfast, 1945

Among the throng of children and mums
who crowd the street for the photograph,
amid the Union bunting and tapered flags,
there's Betty, my auntie, five years old,
swinging her feet and playing hand-games
with girls on a row at the front;
Uncle Stewartie, up at the back,
every inch the corner boy
with his Cagney tough-guy pose
in a window-ledge.
My granny stares from left to right
to where my dad
half-squats on a wooden box,
late, barefoot, his face a knot
of fear and faked enthusiasm.
He's out of sync,
he doesn't fit now war is won

As if he could hear already
his daddy's footsteps
from half a continent away,
homeward bound
with jokes and hugs,
serrated knife in his Army kitbag,
demob pay and a thirst for oblivion
no distillery could match.

After the Riot

The teapot still touch-warm from hours before,
slops of leaves in cups and tumblers whisky-wet
where I now wiped my finger, tasted life, that heated life
that hurried in for refuge through the door.
Ashtrays packed, some butts half-smoked
and cirrus of last night's smoke where loud hushed talk
was not supposed to stir the little ones upstairs.
Black-stained clothes lay dumped on a chair,
their smell stretched from the front room to back gate
where others had slipped homewards after dark.
While adults slept, I took their empty space
as if enacting my small part in a wordless pact.
I washed the cups and glasses, emptied butts
and threw the bloodied tissues in the grate.

Homing

There was always a nervy flutter
in Davey's fingers as he held his pigeons
but it would calm   just moments later
as seeds were pecked from his upturned palms
and he felt the tucked assurance of their wings.
"You can feel their heartbeats thrumming," he'd say
as he smoothed his cheek to the breast
and glided a racer into my hands.
I loved those Saturday hours of watching him
with his birds in paintbook hues of blue and grey
and coded coos. His breath by then
was whiskey-thick but that smelled too
of his gentle strangeness – barefoot
down the yard to the coop to show his favourites,
his scramble of hair like red wire-wool.
I couldn't guess how much
that stretch of yard walled out the past
or quarantined what he couldn't
stutter to admit. We heard
it was his pal Terry's death-throes
at a Cyprus border post that set him off
then demob-drunk and adrift back home
and never quite right after that
except out there with his Black Diamonds until
that worst of summers

and he was gone,
burnt out from the mixed estate,
his wee roost turned to ash.
Warned the night before by a Catholic feller
he'd once done a favour for work
"Davey, you never heard this from me . . ."
he turned his pigeons loose to the mountain skies,
fled with his suitcase on the afternoon boat,
stumbled from tremor to shakes
on tarmac-gangs from Merseyside to Birmingham.
I turfed up twenty or so years later
and he was still padding about barefoot,
swerved a spilling mug of tea into my palm
as he gazed out from another back door.
Homing with nothing to hold.

Brewing Up

When the sports teacher/careers adviser took one look at me
and said *You're tall, have you thought of joining the Army?*
I knew it was over already. For the next ten minutes
of his required consultation so I could be ticked as seen
he advised a factory apprenticeship
because it was *good for your dad*
then asked, from auto script, what I liked doing.
I told him I read the kind of books
the school library didn't stock,
I said I'd like to write books they didn't teach at school.
And when he sneered *So where do you see yourself
ten years from now?* I spotted the Silver Jubilee mug
on his desk, thought of the living and dead,
names and ideas he couldn't fathom,
a book I'd just been reading and said
I'd like to be supping tea with Brendan Behan.

To the Young Woman Who Wrote Her Number on My Left Thigh on the Nightclub Stairs, Cushendall, Sept. 1994

If I hadn't been so hasty to take a shower
I'd've called, you'd've been home,
I'd be on a train to Dublin the next weekend,
we'd have met under Clerys Clock
and you'd have mistaken me briefly
for someone exotic,
introduced me to your five brothers as a friend
you were showing round town.
We'd have inter-railed
and slept on beer-sticky floors,
you'd have fled your horrified parents
so we could share a flat in Camden.
By now we'd have our own
fridge magnet collection,
hate each other,
you'd be blaming me
for the baby out of marriage
that heaped eternal shame
on your god-fearing folks back home,
we'd be getting divorced,
feuding over money and the kid.
Or by some unlikely fluke of luck
one of us might be well-paid,
we'd be making an annual pilgrimage
to Cushdendall where we'd get pissed in Johnnie-Joe's,

you'd make a ritual
of writing on my inner thigh –
or someone else's thigh,
a young feller's who skipped the shower
and took the train to Dublin.
I'll catch you on the rebound.

Delirium in the Rex Bar

By the time Big Molly took the stage
she was so shit-faced she had
to coat-hang herself off the mic-stand;
tried to speak but couldn't
so she wailed the ballad
of Billy McFadzean
as if the words were so deep-sponged
she could sweat them off her tongue.

All hearts were broken
before she'd turned a line
because we knew that song
so well, half-dead
we could sing along.
But for those minutes,
her arms outstretched and imploring,
oozing make-up or tears –
it was hard to tell –
Molly could've been a stray chanteuse,
a Piaf, her fag-raddled soprano
thematic to the bar-room's
stinky mist of whiskey and Harp.

What did it matter
in our drunken trance
that we were mouthing
an anthem

about a young feller
who threw himself on a bomb,
left so little of himself
there was nothing to hang his V.C. on?
History, myth and melody blurred
til Billy could've been in the crowd
or shouting us on
from his shrine
a century later
to stick one on the Hun.

Weeping Molly
squealed a last note
before she tripped
off-stage to beg for gin,
the last of us fell outdoors
and even
as the pub door slammed
I heard that song repeating
in my skull like delirium.

Rise and Fall

That should be Rosa Luxemburg up there
watching over city squares. Children
should gaze at her and wonder, not
Queen Victoria, empress of bloody maps.

That should be John Hewitt, poet,
on Stormont's spacious path, not
Carson grasping at skies
to suffocate Ulster in its past.

That should be Wilfred Owen
and Helen Crawfurd, not
Churchill and Kitchener,
mythologised psychopaths.

That should be the Unknown Miner,
not soulless wasted bronze of Thatcher;
that should be two great Marys on high:
Shelley and Wollstonecraft.

Here come John McLean and Rosas
Luxemburg and Parks, they rise
where Dundas, Colston, all the others
fall to history's task.

Paper Trail

When I saw them first they weren't in the ground,
they grew out of old men's blazers.
Next I read the death-black head
of the buttonhole reading 'Haig'
and I wondered why the living would boast
the name of one who sent young factory lads
by the street-load to their death-throes.

They bloomed on the lapels of men and women
so mealy-mouthed they couldn't tell of killing
except in camouflage of words like thanks and sacrifice.
They propagated every year
so ritually and so certainly
they were as seasonal as toffee apple.
From Falklands, Ireland to Iraq
those poppies reached so seamlessly
you'd think we were the ones –
not paper petals – made for war.

And every year their bloom-time lengthened.
Poppies branded news presenters,
poppies drugged to acquiescence all who watched them blow.
A million reddened beautifully to form a sculpted moat,
the orchestrated howling of Joss Stone was such
the heavens might emote; the poppies bowed as one
because war loves charity loves money loves war
and children need to be taught it's their turn next.

To the Lit-Fest Organisers
of an Event by Alastair Campbell

Whenever I hear him choking the airwaves
or he clogs the columns of *The Independent*
with talk of his war with depression
I think of those who can never tune in
or share the distinction of his words:
the choked, the incinerated, orphaned
or those who died, beyond anyone's gaze,
of trauma, wounds and malnutrition.
The ones for whom *war* is more than a few keystrokes.
And then I start to multiply.

I think of his audience's faces,
attentive, vaguely critical and mild
in their accommodating liberalism
and how he must thank them
but mostly thank his hosts
for these charmed chances to tell his story
and leave those other stories to oblivion.

The Second Goal

World Cup quarter-final, England v Argentina, 1986.

i.m. Diego Maradona

Four years after
Belgrano's
sailors
burned
and drowned,
'Gotcha'
screamed
across
Britain's
news-stands,
conscripts
shuddered
in ratholes
and bragging
Maggie's
army
cruised home,
he outmanoeuvres
defences
like an avenger
out for a stroll.
All their flags
are upended
as feet of god
roll in that goal.

Imperia

One day when you least expect it,
when you have almost forgotten
how your cartographers executed lines on the map,
this ghost will appear in irreconcilable form,
a beautiful-grotesque creation of your past.
Those measurements scored by your predecessors,
those lines will hair-trigger right back.

A Union flag in the oily Atlantic
where its inhabitants salute
your remotest godhead in their sleep?
A desert storm, a Suez pact,
the very notion of yourself
polluted by myth-made longevity?
It could've been any of these,
or tanks and flag burnt black
that led to your unravelling –

But fittingly it is this, the nondescript:
a demarcation thread that runs through village lanes
to sever kith and glens from sea to sea,
a line that can't be folded into schoolbook history.
This is your neighbour's payback,
neither bomb nor armed revolt
but line of turf you can't horse-trade,
treaty you can't unpack.

Did you suppose this was just your heritage-spoil
or you could ride hysteria's waves then jolly on home,
did you imagine hubris as bad P.R.,
your conquests as old cast-offs left untracked?

This was your first, will be your last,
a sliced-up crop of land that soils
your addiction to yourself.
You poked this ghost, Britannia,
be thankful it is more sparing than your least act.

Grosvenor Square, London

There was this feller, a dad he was.
Don't ask me why he was there
but not to protest against war, I'm guessing,
unless a sleeping bairn in a pram was his covert weapon,
because just as the riot broke out and people
were scattering, charging, surging, trampling everywhere
and smoke bombs thickened, flames were rising
and up on the wall of the US embassy three masked
demonstrators were strutting, burning the Stars and Stripes
to the roar and salutes of the crowd, and just
as we could hear the first incoming clatter of hooves
he was right in front of me, lifting the pram.
And me and two women without any prompting
grabbed an end each and hoisted the wean
– still sleeping through the whole shebang –
onto the pavement beside the side-street
and then the dad was shouting, stranded,
so all of us lifted him, he was crowd-surfed
to the edge of the riot, and smiling, laughing,
thanking us as he was planted down with his child
then hurrying off from the scene.
And that was the instant I hunched down low
just in time to miss the shattering glass from the pub windows
and the Robocops as they zig-zagged on the street
and swiped through bodies and smoke;

and it makes me wonder, these many years later,
why it was so easy to lift a small child
backwards in a pram through a riot
when millions, millions of us, couldn't stop a war.

The Night that Peace Broke Out

Sammy and Conor gatecrashed U2,
swerved invisibly past the security guards,
while I ripped my trousers
and nearly my bollocks scaling 10-foot rails;
but who needed Bono or even a band
when there were settees on pavements
all over the wilder corners of Belfast,
the big-screen music was always in range,
ghetto-blasters and braziers
took over side-streets
and the Lagan banks ribboned through the dark
for me like a guiding soul.
I bought 20 Rothmans from a car-boot chancer,
handed £10 to a kid just because he asked,
and before I'd hit midnight's last orders
was floating down Great Victoria Street
as if I was drunk on the very air,
trapeze of lights and noise and revellers.
And it was there, mid-pavement, right there
I paused and kissed a beaming woman
in polka dot green as she leaned in
at the same fluked glance to me;
We said thank-you then left. That's all.
Thanks for exultant memory.

The Rewrite

This time it didn't go to script.
The Army cadets were well turned out,
Marines were looking hard and sharp,
The RAF were pin-smart blue,
Legion veterans jangled by
to seats beside the podium.
Wreaths were fingered in readiness,
a bugler lad was well rehearsed
and a good turnout of young to old
were looking their best sad-solemn.
Then as the Bishop took the mic
to read "At the going down of the Sun"
there came a screech of ear-busting feedback;
a crack-crack-crack of the monument names
and through the gaps repulsive forms -
the Remembered - in their death throes.
Those who'd been named-checked
so determinedly for a century or more
were back for a personal show:
A conscript juggled his innards
as he wailed in a young lad's face,
a volunteer clawed the Bishop's legs
with skin and clothes ablaze
while in the back row a Navy gunner
had got the Women's Institute in his sights
and was staging a silent rigamortis protest.

The Lady Provost puked on her robes,
two veterans keeled over dead,
Paras wept, reporters begged
forgiveness, a Black Watch sergeant fled.
Within two minutes the whole assembly
threw down their poppies, renounced the past:
the ghosts dispersed. Where there had been
a monument now was grass.

Making a Homeland

for Jacqueline

A sick and ageing Labrador in the car's back seat,
boot stuffed with clothes and £65 to our name,
at least we've got giros to claim
and your pal's empty house to use as our own,
spare time to write best-sellers
after I flicked a V to another take-the-piss boss
with his largesse of *extending your short-term contract*.
Not much to show at forty-five for a supposed career
but maverick honour exacts a price
and here in the layby I'm glad we've taken the shot:
The car, at least, is paid for and, hey, open-top –
the spoils of a well-paid job in your previous life –
and there is this sign saying
Welcome to Scotland/Failte Gu Alba
and for a while as we inhale crisp April air
infused with wet grass and heather
we're magnetised by something new,
expelling residual strains of what we've left,
those cold migrations of the past:
childhood ferry journeys, evictions,
demos, pickets, checkpoints and the dole.
We're scattered: that's our inheritance. So strange
to our roots that our names could be accidents,
now lugging our pans by Vorschprungdonkey,
feeling rich for a day on last month's pay.

I say I'm tired of being bounced from city to town,
chasing dead-end jobs, not knowing where
or for how I'll belong. You give me a look;
and in those minutes we seal the unwritten pact
that will sustain us: this is our Rubicon;
foot to the floorboard and no going back
by anyone's curse or demand.
Though we might be from everywhere else,
we're of that mongrel band who make/remake
our kith and clan. And we will do that in this land.

Snap

I'm watching my eight-year-old daughter
as she plays on the harbour beach
and it is so ordinary, this joyfulness.
She skips the boat ropes, hurdles sandcastles,
pulls a Gargoyle face for a summery snap.

I zoom but pause: I'm reeling back
to a girl who would've been her age
smiling shyly beside the beach road
in Rafah, 2003. Her dad looks on,
so pleased outsiders stopped to talk,
and his daughter beams because
the pose and a photograph are so rare.

I'm thinking of that shot
and spot where two days later
an Israeli shell incinerated a water butt
and killed two children about her age.
My girl smiles back.
She cannot know I'm wondering
if that Rafah girl is grown-up now,
her own child playing
or did not make it
beyond click-click a snap.

Eleven o Clocks

i.m. Dorothy Young

I see her first through the frosted-glass partition
of the hall to kitchen, sliding her feet
bobble-slippered over a blue-tiled floor,
click-tick-clicking the paraffin heater. I smell
the thin escape of fume, eidetic, warm. It ignites.
Then I am there too, about four, at the table,
legs kicking mid-air. She pushes two custard creams
on a plate to my hands, I slurp diluted orange juice
from a Tupperware beaker with a chewed rim
where my two older brothers had drank before, pre-school.
She flicks the radio on. Petula is singing Downtown,
mam's singing too *Listen to the rhythm of the gentle bossa nova*
though she hasn't seen a dance floor in years. She's always
in the background, doing, tending, until she is there no more.

Miniature

My parents bought this armchair miniature
of Causeway rock from an old shawled woman
who chiselled it out of the Giant's steps;
she was what passed in 1960 for a tourist trap.
They must've smiled, new husband and bride
on her first trip to the Glens,
turning it over in their hands
and wrapping it in newspaper
when they packed their suitcase
in the B&B at Portrush
for the drive back to Belfast.
They gave it favoured status
in their first council house,
next to the wedding photograph
on the rented Rediffusion TV,
and it went with them
from terraced home to semi,
cities to towns as sons were raised, departed,
wherever they made a mantelpiece.
I claim it now as a bungalow's cleared,
hold the edge they held from fifty million years before,
before the visitor centre,
the picture-book yarns of Finn McCool,
when there was only an old shawled woman
halfway up the cliffs.
This rock is all that now exists
as if they too were myth.

What You Leave
i.m. Tommy Young

You are turning invisible now. As if through cataracts.
Once you were as sharp as a kipper tie among Sunday best,
you smelled of oil and welding-scorch
that twined the overalls you wore like second skin,
you sang as you shaved, your eyes were Atlantic blue,
your brogue was unsieved, you laughed because
it was the exuberance that surfaced
the other side of hunger, war and work.
But now that's all confined to photographs.
Obscured to lineage. How much is left?
I think of this: how you sat smiling, eating ice-cream
the morning after they snatched you back from the dead
although you knew you'd be gone in days.
Far more than parting words, this said
don't be afraid. That's how you lived.
These things you leave invisibly when you go.

Clock of the World

The clock on the wall of the Market Bar
Hasn't changed since I came in.
I know it must be accurate because
my universe is the same
as when I drank that first Lagavulin
and the news headlines
are the same, on loop between
the nags and scores, big screen.
I know it's 6.15pm
although my watch says going-home time
because I'm wearing a cheap Timex
whereas the clock above the bar
looks like it's seen a war or two,
and performed heroic service
and that is good enough for me.
My watch is like
the clock of the world
that's always overwound
or in the dark whereas
the clock on the wall of the Market Bar
is nicotine-stained in 2020,
it's poised in oval symmetry
above the refracted glint
of the Guinness pumps
and it is synchronised
to peace and love
and communal harmony.

This Harbour

Though no-one can possess it
this is your harbour:
breakwater, ancient stones, clock tower,
slipway, sands and lanes, braes and coves,
Pictish ruins to Covenanters' cross,
the war memorial scratched on a hilly skyline,
Dunnottar Castle where Scotland's jewels
were smuggled out under a quine's coarse frock
to dodge Cromwell's shock-troops
and centuries later film directors
etch silhouettes across the remainder of walls.
All of this is yours, from ice-cream shop
to faery pools; topography,
history, ghosts and customs too,
known or neglected, dormant under rocks
or snagged on nets, buried under silted tiers
of dead fish and the footprints of millennia.
Fog and the way the sunlight flashes
over the inner harbour water in summer
until the last buckets and spades are gone
and children leave no more than ghosts of play, are yours.
They were yours from the day
you shivered homewards in a scratchy towel
and will be yours even when you are gone;
they are indented now by
memory's invisible ink
 as you are too on them.

Freed Verse

When this is all over
there will be no more hellish poetry readings.
Eight-year-old girls will not be required
to accompany dads to listen to grey
soft-spoken people attempting to be
profound in verse.

There will be socialism,
homes with a garden for all,
picnics, parties, more home-working,
a universal declaration of the rights of the dog,
climate change will be halted
and boring poetry readings will be outlawed.
Francine, instead of dreary hushed evenings
in libraries and coffee shops
there will be free-for-alls:
book shop karaoke and face-paintings fests.
Most of all, noise.

The only poems allowed in public
will be about Pokemons. All others
will be stuffed in a drawer.
Poets who breach the new rules
will be quarantined, made to eat their epics.
The rest, although they may not admit it,
will thank their gods, or muse,
that they are finally liberated.

The Haar

Fog enfolds us at summer's peak.
We might as well be islanded here at the harbour's edge,
waiting for something, god knows what,
to signal over the wall from out of the haar.
This mist has thickened for four days now,
the evening lights remind me of impressionist prints;
when I trudge out in wellies, the dog
runs on, as if we're scouting the out-of-reach
before the inevitable – we beat a retreat
and like all living things are entranced by the fire.
Here it's easy to tell yourself the world's your friend,
everyone's drunk or asleep
and wake to find the bay's last light snuffed out,
the clocks don't count, we're folded within and without,
then tap a screen for latest news, up close
of wars and demons on the approach.

A Whistling Kettle

Between the office boxroom and the kitchen
as I pad in Superman slippers for biscuits and tea
America's wailing. It's got my lugs
in a pincer movement between
the TV in the big bedroom and one in the lounge
and it's wailing 'hope' and 'freedom'
and 'dreams' as if those words
were copyrighted but coming out new.
There are 195 countries in the world
according to latest counts
but for now America's wailing,
a poet wails about 'light',
an old man manages to read his script
and a singer emotes
so nowhere else is news
unless the dog steps on the remote
and tunes into Al-Jazeera.
And then the unexpected-expected happens:
the kettle is whistling on the gas hob,
it's hollering like a siren through the fog
of hope and freedom and dreams and light
that drown out awkward notions of war
and how those words are its hymnsheet;
and the whistling kettle is my here and now,
my channel-hopper that shatters the spell
between the office boxroom and the kitchen
as everything goes Gaga.

A Door

I know what's meant by *never go back,*
leave the past freeze-framed, intact.
I knocked once at the door of my childhood home
but no-one came. The morning paper
was stuffed in the letterbox,
the step's red paint was faint and scratched,
an ornamental windmill spun on the grass,
everything was so ordinary. Calm.
But I was only a trespasser there,
gazing through frosted glass to where
my mother might be, still clutching a taytie knife,
the key in her apron pocket   fingertip-warm.

Here to There

Fog on the braes
draws me to where I come from.
If I could climb through it
would I return to where
the rain comes off
the Black Mountain in sheets
and time is punctuated still
by a factory's horn?
The street would be hushed on Sunday
while in the living room
The Seekers would sing at 33rpm,
there'd be a newspaper open on the table
with headlines telling of riots
on the next estate,
Bestie's new landlady,
The Bomb, and Life in Pictures
of the First Man on the Moon.
Somewhere between these extremities
I'd dream. The Moon
would be more reachable to me
than braes I now call home.

Lightning Source UK Ltd.
Milton Keynes UK
UKHW042357291121
394787UK00001B/59